Introduction

My husband, Josh, and I have been through a lot in our marriage, some very painful and hopeless situations. We have watched our marriage be restored by the Creator of the universe from a very broken place. The ramblings of my heart on these pages are truly out of having been through the fire and from what I have learned while in the fire and anyone who knows me well knows that this is truly from the Holy Spirit. At the beginning of our trials, the Lord told me that He was going to use what I was going through for other women and marriages. I tucked that promise in my heart, not knowing how or when that would happen and many detours and 8 years later, I heard Him say, "it is time to tell your story!" The Lord laid on my heart to start sending out by text or email to women a 30 day prayer challenge for their husbands/marriage. God burdened my heart for our husbands. The Lord showed me a new perspective, and has given me a glimpse into the battles our men face. He allowed me to better understand that they are fighting their minds, hearts, and bodies daily, and we don't need to be one of their battles. So I started sending these daily challenges with commentary to some friends and my sisters and the Lord began to lay women on my heart, one by one, women I wouldn't have thought of myself and they were receptive and then they began to ask if I could add their sisters, moms, friends, ect and it has grown into a texting/emailing ministry. I have been blown away at the responses and encouragement and testimonies that I have received from some of these women. God is so AMAZING! He did it in such a way that I couldn't have imagined it. A texting ministry? Where I told women to have grace and compassion on men? It is almost comical to me how He used my greatest fear, trial and weaknesses and turned them into an avenue to minister to other wives and women. My story is truly a beauty from ashes story and yours will be too! Hang in there and do not grow weary in doing good for at the proper time you will reap a harvest if you do not give up [Galatians 6:9] A verse that I clung to during our trials was from James 1:12 and it says "Blessed are those who persevere in trials for when they have stood the test then they will receive the crown of life!" IM finally on the Beauty side of these ashes and the Sun finally rose from my dark nights and I am LIVING PROOF that these verses are TRUTH!

There is much more to my story, but I believe there are more chapters or books to come. At least that is what the Lord is telling me, so again I will wait for His leading! To God be the Glory!

I am so thankful that you have chosen to be a part of this project and I'm so excited about what God will do with the rest of my story and yours.

Much Love Always,

Haley

Day 1:

I want to preface the first day by telling you this whole book thing and sharing the depths of my heart with strangers is totally out of my comfort zone but one that The Lord didn't nudge me to do but literally burdened my heart with a pain in my chest -so I knew I had to be obedient to him. You will have to get used to my writing, it is not formal and it's the Lord speaking through me, a broken vessel, who rambles a bit too much and has no PhD or formal training, it's just me talking to you my friend, over a cup of coffee. Because this started as a texting ministry, it's a very texty language and sometimes I make up words- bear with me and set aside my faults if you will, and just let the Lord speak to your heart! My husband, Josh and I were the most in love couple you had ever seen and then my fairytale world came crashing down one day and we spent years trying to recover, years co-existing, fighting, barely breathing it felt like at times and little by little as we pressed in to the Lord and pressed on in the Good fight and stood the test of our trial, the Lord revived our hearts and restored our marriage and we are back to being the most in love couple you have ever seen and grossing people out IM sure but I want you to know, every word that comes out of my mouth and through my typing fingers is either from being in the refiner's fire or from coming out of the fire. I never want anyone to think I've got it all together [I definitely DO NOT] or we have a perfect marriage because we are still broken souls in need of our savior, but we have fought very hard to have the marriage we now have, one that has been restored by the creator of the universe from that very broken place. I give GOD all the glory for what we have learned and are still learning along the way. If any of these daily prayer challenge thingies [you will learn really quick there is no eloquence in my speech and I do not claim to have used all of the best words available] but if these daily challenges prompt you to have questions, comments or a need for prayer. I would be so happy to pray for you. I'm so excited that you've agreed to be a part of this challenge. I pray that your marriage goes deeper and your love for The Lord and each other grows deeper than it ever has. Ps-day 1 is EASY ☺

Pray that your husband will grow in his spiritual walk and that he will guard his heart by developing spiritual disciplines Bible reading and study, prayer and scripture memorization, etc. [2 Peter 3:18 Prov. 4:23]

"And the Lord will guide you continually and satisfy your desire in scorched places and make your bones strong and you shall be like a watered garden, like a spring of water, whose waters do not fail" Isaiah 58:11

Day 2

Prayer is so powerful in our marriages. I want to just say a prayer for each of you as we walk through this challenge together.

Father God,

I want to start today by thanking you for each woman who has agreed to be part of this challenge. Lord, I pray that you would soften our hearts towards our husbands. Help us to see our husbands as you see them and help us to have grace on our husbands. Lord I know you want to work out your plan in each of our marriages and you desire that our marriage honor you. I thank you Father for these women who are willing to take a challenge of praying daily, specific and earnest prayers for their husbands for 30 days. I know you are faithful to reveal yourself to us even though we don't know what you have planned for us during this journey. I ask that we would open our hearts to be receptive to what you have for each of us. In Jesus name, Amen!

SIT on this verse if you will today and think of how you can exemplify this today and THROUGHOUT THIS CHALLENGE—this will be our theme verse throughout the entire challenge!

"She brings him good, not harm, all the days of her life."

Proverbs 31:12

Pray that your husband's relationship with God and his word will bear fruit in his life. Pray that he will be a man of wisdom and understanding, fearing The Lord.

[Prov. 3:7, 9:10]

Praise the LORD! How joyful are those who fear the LORD and delight in obeying his commands. Psalm 112:1

Day 3-

Man sometimes I need to sit on a verse for more than a day like really sit and let the hard hearted places of my heart absorb it-sometimes it take more than a day, sometimes many, many days, the verse I gave you yesterday is one of them. As I was pondering this verse-I just heard The Lord saying- can you imagine if wives really did this for their husbands? Can you imagine what a different marriage we would have if it was our goal to protect our man's heart and do him good, build him up around others, especially other women and not just In public but in private too. We so often think they don't need it or we are afraid they will get all cocky and big headed [I'll admit, that idea paralyzed me for years and years in our relationship] I was so afraid If I told him how much I adored him, it would make me look weak and then he would think he was so awesome and he would realize he was too awesome for me. Sounds so stupid but it crippled me. Maybe that isn't your issue but I know as wives we could all do better at "doing our man good, not harm, all the days of our life" not for anything in return but for simply and joyfully wanting to do your man good! So if you need to sit on one verse for days and days and really let it wash over your heart-guess what???? That's ok -there's no rule about a new verse each day.

Pray that your husband will be able to feel conviction and mourn over his sin, that he would confess and repent. Pray that his heart will be softened toward the Lord. [Ps. 51:2-4, 7-9; Micah 6:8]

Day 4

Pray that your husband will become a fearless leader in your home Pray that he will lead you wisely and love you unconditionally, so that God will be glorified in your marriage. [Eph. 5:25-29, 1 Peter 3:7, 1 Corinthians 11:3, 1 Corinthians 14:3]

Ladies we are called to submit to our husband and respect him -OUCH in this age of I AM WOMAN HEAR ME ROAR-it's easy to ignore the idea of a gentle and quiet spirit or being submissive or respectful and boy do I know about this issue. The Lord has been speaking these words to me, sometimes I don't get it all the first time I hear it which is why I say "speaking" and not "spoken" Here is what he is saying "Haley why do you try to be the leader of your home? I have made him the leader, but he can't be if you keep trying to TAKE CONTROL. This is not your battle sweet girl, this is my warrior son's battle-Lay it down at my feet"

A man sometimes won't step up when we are "controlling" everything and we are so scared to let him do it for FEAR he may fall but I do believe and have seen that when we walk beside him encouraging him in his role of leader, building him up and letting him be the man God created him to be-he will step up to the plate! Let go of control today -step back and let your man Lead!

As we pray these things for our husbands, I hope we will also pray some

of them for ourselves. As we desire to be loved unconditionally, so let us love unconditionally and sacrificially and not because we want anything in return but because it gives us joy when we give to our man. Sometimes we are so focused on how all the ways our husbands are Messing up or not what we want in different areas or didn't meet our expectations, the list goes on and on of how they aren't meeting our needs but truly when we take the focus off of what they aren't doing and
1-focus on the good they ARE doing and 2-look at our own lives and ask God to reveal our sin, only THEN the glasses we are looking through begin to change and his "issues" aren't so horrible or God gives us love for that annoying thing he does and wait for it- we might actually begin to see it as cute -or we have compassion and grace for the sin that he may be trapped in. I pray that God is doing a great thing in your marriage today. Reviving it or restoring it!

Day 5-

❤Pray that your husband will be faithful to his wedding vows. Pray that he will have a desire to cultivate your relationship as a sign of his loyalty and commitment to you, and as a picture of Christ's love for the Church. [Prov. 20:6 Heb. 13:4, Eph. 5:33, Numbers 30:2, Gen. 2:24]❤ ps and kiss him when he gets home

Ok these first few days have been sweet prayers for our man but we are about to dive into some Issues that might be hard to even read, pray, think about, ect. I urge you to ask The Lord today during your prayer for your husband to also prepare YOUR heart for the rest of the challenge. As with any challenge it isn't all easy. It may reveal a wounded area of your life, marriage and/or heart but don't give up because God wants those parts of your heart. He wants the hidden, hush hush, don't let anyone know, wear a mask to cover it, wounded and walled up parts of your precious heart! Ask and then allow the Holy Spirit to fill you up with Grace and compassion for your husband as you pray the prayers that may get hard. He doesn't want our Put together self, the one we put on for church. He wants the messy, the weaknesses, the impurities, the weary, the hopeless parts, the anger and the pain. He wants to take your ashes, your husband's ashes and your marriage's ashes and make something beautiful for his glory!

Isaiah 61:1-3

The Spirit of the Sovereign Lord is on me, because the Lord has anointed me to proclaim good news to the poor.

He has sent me to bind up the brokenhearted, to proclaim freedom for the captives and release from darkness for the prisoners, to proclaim the year of the Lord's favor and the day of vengeance of our God, to comfort all who mourn, and provide for those who grieve in Zion—to bestow on them a crown of beauty instead of ashes, the oil of joy instead of mourning, and a garment of praise instead of a spirit of despair. They will be called oaks of righteousness, a planting of The Lord for the display of his splendor. AMEN!

Day 6

Pray that your husband will love righteousness and hate wickedness, especially the evils of the culture. Pray that he will recognize and avoid wickedness in his own life, and if necessary, take a clear, strong stand against evil. [Ephesians 6:12-13, John 17:15 1 Cor. 10:12-13]

Even in our attempt to live an upright life, we can get deceived into wickedness. We can find creative ways to justify wickedness and it's just what the enemy is trying to do-keep us so busy in our "doing good" that we justify our sin or anything that draws us away from our relationship with the Father. The Father, the Creator of the universe desires a relationship more than religion from us. He is jealous for us and he will do whatever it takes to bring his son or daughter back to him. Are we so busy ministering to others that we aren't ministering to our man? Maybe we aren't ministering to anyone at all, quite frankly maybe you are hard hearted towards the Lord right now, maybe you are angry and bitter and you are walking in blatant wickedness. Listen I have been there too, unfortunately, and bitterness and hard hearts lead to wickedness. The Lord is calling you home and he wants to rescue you and restore to you the joy of your salvation. Ask the Lord to give your husband brokenness for his sin and the wicked ways that might be in his heart so that he might come to walk closer in relationship with the Father. And HEY while you are before the throne of God, ask him to search your heart as well!

search me Oh God and know my heart, test me and know my anxious thoughts, see if there is any offensive way in me and lead me in the way everlasting. Psalms 139:23-24

Day 7

Pray that your husband will safeguard his heart against inappropriate relationships with the opposite sex. Pray that his heart will be pure and undivided in his commitment to you. [Prov. 6:23-26 Rom. 13:14]
There is power in prayer, especially in this area of our man's life that is sometimes something we don't want to think about or we say oh he's just being a man or my man doesn't struggle with that.

David was called a man after Gods own heart, yet he struggled in this area by lusting over his bathing neighbor and then having an inappropriate relationship with her. In Job 1:31, Job says I have made A Covenant with my eyes to not look lustfully at a woman. I used to really think that if my man was looking lustfully at a woman it was because I was not good enough. Yall please hear me here, because I think so many women struggle in this area. I have just in the last couple years begun to understand that this truly is "every man's battle" this goes back to our biblical heroes of the bible. While we can't take away their battle, I have watched what happens when our men commit to make a covenant with their eyes. They cannot do it in their own will but only through the strength of God. I was always so afraid to talk about this issues with my husband, but bringing to light these things and talking honestly about these things has allowed such freedom and I now am able to tell my husband thank you for making the covenant with his eyes and relying on The Lord to follow through on the covenant and for having amazing self-control. The Lord can handle this subject and wants us to lift up our men in this battle, to not keep it off limits, to talk about it and bring it to light. This world constantly throws itself at our man's eyes and WE can be on our knees for our men because it is such a battle for them.

Therefore I tell you, whatever you ask in prayer, believe that you have received it, and it will be yours. Mark 11:24

Trying to wrap this up although I could probably go on and on [not surprising☺] but In another regard 2 things as women to help men and our men in the battle,

1-pray that we would not be the woman described in Proverbs 6:23-26 or Prov. 5:6-14

2-Pray that we would fulfill our mans sexual needs and desires and give him the intimacy that he craves and not withhold ourselves from him.

She Does Him Good by: Haley Bates

Day 8

Pray that your husband will work hard to provide for your family, to the best of his ability. Pray that the Lord would provide him with God honoring characteristics in his career and that his success would be defined by his character—Integrity, honesty, decisiveness, strength, an analytical mind, persistence, organizational skills, God-honoring relationships with people and determination. [Rom. 12:9-21 1 Cor. 15:58]

Ok, some men have got this down pat-maybe to the point of being a workaholic, Some men struggle with integrity, laziness, finishing a job or quitting too soon or never being satisfied or some might be happy in their career, but it's hardly enough to cover the minimum family bills. Whatever the situation may be in your family, lift your man up in this area. Sometimes we nag in this area or put in what we think he should do or express that what he is doing is not Good enough.. This is an area of our man's life where he needs our support and belief in him and ultimately we trust in The Lord to work out the details. It's amazing what happens when a man knows you stand behind him and support him no matter what happens at his job or with his clients or with your bank account. I have definitely struggled in this area in the past and the Lord is teaching me a lot about standing beside my man no matter what. His HEART is more important than all of the monetary, the what other people will think, the failure or success at work, the way you love your husband and encourage his heart is eternal! Does he know that no matter what happens you will stand by him? That's a hard question to ask ourselves.

But encourage one another daily, as long as it is called "Today," so that none of you may be hardened by sin's deceitfulness. Hebrews 3:13

Psalm 101:1-2 - I will sing of steadfast love and justice to you, O LORD, I will make music. I will ponder the way that is blameless. Oh when will you come to me? I will walk with integrity of heart within my house.

Day 9

Pray that your husband will speak words that build you and your family up, and reflect a heart of love. [Prov. 18:21]

This ultimately comes down to speaking life -pray that his words or your words into him would speak life, build each other up and encourage each other. In Ephesians 4:29 the word says "Do not let any unwholesome talk come out of your mouths, but only what is helpful for building others up according to their needs, that it may benefit those who listen!" The word also says that OUR words can speak life and take life, can save our lives or ruin our lives [Prov. 18:21, 13:3]

How many of us as women have experienced both the repercussions of the words we speak or the fruit of the words we speak and how about from others -every single one of us have been hurt by words at one time or we have been lifted up by someone's words! I know I have failed in this area many times! If we want to be encouraged and spoken life to, we should speak life and pray that life, encouragement and edification would be spoken in our homes and out of our hearts and mouths.

From out of our mouth flows that which is in our heart (Matthew 12:34)

An anxious heart weighs a man down, but a kind word cheers him up. Proverbs 12:23

Day 10

Pray that your husband will cultivate strong integrity, and not compromise his convictions. Pray that his testimony will be genuine, that he will be honest in his business dealings, and will never do anything that he needs to hide from others. [Prov. 20:7 1 Tim. 1:5, 3:7 Eph. 6:10-12]

This can be a real temptation for men in small dealings or in large Dealings. When he may give in to a temptation at work or in his business dealings to be unethical or dishonest, it can take your entire family out from under Gods umbrella of protection. That's a scary place to be. God is a part of every detail of our life and our husband's life. He sees what we do when we think no one is watching. We should definitely pray in advance for this specific prayer but IF your husband has failed in this area recently or in the past, be Jesus to him and give him grace, mercy and unconditional love and continue to support him even when he has messed up. THAT is the trenches of marriage and -loving each other through the trenches will result in a more intimate and deeper marriage relationship than you can imagine! Show your husband you love him today -if it means biting your tongue in a conversation or giving him a hug when he walks through the door. Tell him you support him no matter what happens. Don't do it for what you will receive, just do it for his heart only!

Do nothing out of selfish ambition or
vain conceit. Rather, in humility
value others above yourselves.

Philippians 2:3

Day 11

Pray that your husband will have a humble, teachable spirit and a servant's heart before the Lord. Pray that he will listen to God and desire to do His will. [Prov. 15:33 Proverbs 13:18, prov. 11:1-2, Eph. 6:6-8]

I hope that as you are saying these prayers that you

1-Know that it doesn't matter how your prayer sounds or even if it feels cold, pointless or not-applicable to your life -just say it in your own way even if it's while reading the text in a prayer to God. Just say it. He will work out the rest!

2-I hope it will encourage you to not just pray this prayer for your husband but also it would cause you to turn inward and pray the prayer for yourself and your children.

The area of pride is one that I could write parts 1-10 on because I have struggled so long with this issue in my heart. See even that is hard for me to admit to yall-deep breath over here. Pride is such a barrier between our hearts and the Father and also such a barrier to the place of intimacy we desire in our marriages. Sometimes it's the husband's issue of pride but for me this has been a huge part of my life that The Lord has worked out in me and taken me through the refiner's fire many, many times.

God OPPOSES the proud and gives grace to the humble. James 4:6

I don't know about you but I do not want to be opposed by God! In Proverbs 16:5- it says

"The Lord detests the proud of heart. Be sure of this: they will not go unpunished."

YIKES!!! I have to constantly keep my heart in check in the area of pride. There are SO many types of pride. So let's talk about it-what is pride? Pride is when you won't accept someone's gift to you when you really need it. It's thinking you are better than someone else, it's trying to live a fake life and not accept and acknowledge the one you are actually living, its being ashamed of your life or lowly circumstances, it isn't relenting in the point you are trying to make, it's anxiety over not being the best, prettiest, richest, smartest ect because you don't want people to know you aren't all of those things. Pride is always being "right" and never admitting you are wrong. Pride is thinking we are better than others or we don't need God. Pride is thinking we can handle everything on our own. Pride is not wanting to go to church with sinners because we think we have it all together or acting like we are the ones that have it all together at church to appear like we are better. Pride is announcing all of your accomplishments to the world and telling everyone how awesome you are instead of waiting for people to compliment you or for The Lord to affirm your accomplishments. The list goes on and on. Pride comes in so many forms. We must truly go with our raw heart before the

Father and ask him to reveal any ways that our sin is separating us from him in. If you don't know if pride is an issue for you-ask The Lord to show you. The Lord will reveal in a still small voice or sometimes he may make it loud and clear by plucking things out of your life one by one before you can see the sin- that's what he did with me. I recommend listening to the still small voice first! Plucking is No fun! But sometimes that's what it takes for us stubborn, hard hearted, prideful sinners.

3- Maybe the area of the day that we are focusing on is a place your husband has overcome huge obstacles in or is really amazing at. For example, my man IS the MOST humble man I know, so today I'm going to thank The Lord for giving him such a humble spirit and I'm going to ask that he would continue to give him a servants heart and that would God would use this amazing part of his heart for helping others and leading others to Christ.

I hope your day is awesome! Have a thankful and pure heart, be humble today as you desire your man to be humble, give your man a hug, a kiss, words of affirmation and/or more.

When you feel discouraged that you are doing all of this and you see no fruits or no growth or no answered prayers- behold God is working in ways you cannot see and HE IS DOING A NEW Thing [can't help but start singing DC TALK-taking it back old school here] you know he's doing it- who's doing it? God is doing a new thing!!

Forget the former things; do not dwell on the past (ooh this is so hard). See I am doing a NEW thing! Now it springs up, do you not percive it? I am making a way in the desert and streams in the wasteland! AMEN! Isaiah 43:18-1

Day 12

Pray that your husband will yield his sexual drive to the Lord and practice self control. Pray that your sexual intimacy together will be fresh, passionate and a reflection of selfless love. [1Cor. 7:3-5, Song of Solomon 7:10-11]

Some of you may feel weird about asking God to "yield your husband's sex drive to The Lord" what does that even mean? The Lord wants every part of our lives. He created sex and it is a beautiful gift that he has given us but so, so many of us and/or our husbands have struggled in this area of our lives at some point in the past or currently. Every one of us knows the amount of sexual sin and corruptness [If that is a word] in this world, not to mention our own lives, we know that God created sex and he gave it to us inside the walls of our marriage. This is a subject that we could spend 30 days praying on in itself but instead of focusing on all of the sin tied to sex-I just, for a moment, want you to focus your prayer today on asking The Lord to strengthen you and your husband's intimacy in a way that is pleasing to The Lord. I think this looks different to different couples. This may sound really crazy but there have been times when I felt our intimacy has been so beautiful that we felt it was a form of worship of The Lord and other times we have worshipped our intimacy instead of The Lord. We all struggle to have pure minds! Women struggle with this too or maybe you struggle with wanting to even BE intimate, maybe your drive is lacking or you just have a lot of "headaches" but let the Lord lead you in praying these specific prayers over your husband and your marriage:

1-That Father God would fulfill my husband's sexual desires with me and no one/or nothing else.

2-that I would submit my desires to The Lord and that they would only be for my husband and that I would always be willing to satisfy his needs.

3- that our sex life would be pleasing to him and that he would take away the wounds, the sin, the addictions or anything that comes between our intimacy and that The Lord would break the bondage of sin in this area of our marriage and that my husband would continue to keep the covenant he has made with God and with his eyes [and if your husband is still in a cycle of sin or hasn't made the decision to make a covenant with his eyes to not look lustfully at other women or pornography -ask The Lord to press upon his heart the desire to submit this area of his life to him and to come to repentance of these sin. If you want to dive deeper, this is a great article and its part of a series of articles on this subject:

http://www.focusonthefamily.com/marriage/sex-and-intimacy/understanding-your-husbands-sexual-needs/your-husbands-sex-drive-is-gods-gift-to-you

15 Drink water from your own cistern, And fresh
water from your own well. 16 Should your springs be
dispersed abroad, Streams of water in the streets? 17
Let them be yours alone, And not for strangers with
you. 18 Let your fountain be blessed, And rejoice in
the wife of your youth. 19 As a loving hind and a
graceful doe, Let her breasts satisfy you at all
times; Be exhilarated always with her love (Proverbs
5:15-19).

Day 13

Pray that your husband would handle finances wisely, will have discernment concerning budgeting and investments, and will be a good steward of his money in regard to giving to the Lord's work. Pray that money will not become a source of discord in your family. [Prov. 23:4-5 Rom. 12:13 Heb. 13:5]

I'm going to be honest with you, the day I was writing this I was super attacked and I knew it was coming. The enemy attacked me in some of our past issues sneaking up but The Lord reminded me to come to the cross. I can definitely let my emotions take over especially in certain wounded places of my heart when I get fearful or feel rejected. He straight up said here is your Opportunity sweet girl to practice what you've written. - Bathe in scripture today and especially when you are being attacked or feeling weak! The word of The Lord is healing to your bones!!

From the ends of the earth I call to you, I call as my heart grows faint; lead me to the rock that is higher than I psalm 61:2

As I felt Myself began to listen to the voice of truth instead of the voice of lies, I felt his peace wash over me and I was able to be vulnerable with my husband again, instead of my selfish nature of hardening my heart and throwing up a wall. When we are walking with The Lord -the enemy wants to seriously take us out! This is when we have to truly live out the truths that we have heard, said and hidden in our heart! Be ready for the attack!

Hide Gods word in your heart that you may not sin against him! Psalm 119:11

Be self-controlled and alert. Your enemy the devil prowls around like a roaring lion looking for someone to devour. 1 Peter 5:8 (NIV)

She Does Him Good by: Haley Bates

Day 14-HAPPY Day OF LOVE ❤❤❤❤❤❤❤❤❤❤❤❤❤

Pray that your husband will LOVE unconditionally and that he would ever be intoxicated with the Lords love and your love.
[1 Corinthians 13, Psalm 103:2-5, proverbs 5:18-19]

Above all else, LOVE EACH OTHER deeply, for Love covers a multitude of sins! 1peter 4:8

-what else can we say? Time and time again the Word of the Lord speaks on Love-verse after verse on the Fathers love and how to love others and how to love him and our children, our husband, our wife, our neighbor. The recurring theme of the BIBLE IS LOVE. The GREATEST LOVE LETTER ever written is the Bible. If we are looking to figure out how to love -we have the perfect instruction book. When we love unconditionally, some of the other things, the things that seem so important begin to fade away. When we act out of unconditional and selfless love, our whole demeanor changes and those in our household will too. Will we be able to accomplish unconditional, selfless love always? HA! NO! But we can try our best and ask The Lord to teach us how to do that. There was a time in our marriage [too many years in to admit] where I sat down and did inventory of 1 Corinthians 13-Am I patient? Am I kind? Am I humble? Do I envy? Do I honor others or dishonor others? Am I self-seeking [also called selfish]? Am I easily angered? Do I keep a record of wrongs [ouch]? Do I delight in evil or rejoice in truth? Do I ALWAYS protect? Do I always trust? Do I always hope and persevere? Yikes that's a hard list to answer honestly? It's not a list of options you can get 50% you are good. LOVE is ALL of these things. I failed miserably and I realized I didn't truly love. I was selfish and selfishness is the opposite of Love. I still fail daily I'm sure, but Praise God he gives new mercy every morning. Being aware and really asking myself some of these questions in response to my kids or my husband has helped to have better responses and overall a happier family and more peace in my home. Love is a choice NOT a feeling! It is choosing to love when you don't feel like it or when they don't deserve it or when you feel like you deserve more. It is putting others before yourself. Today, I challenge you to use this day as a beginning point in your household and marriage to make this your priority -to LOVE like Christ calls us to love, like he loves us, SELFLESSLY and unconditionally.

We love because he first loved us. 1 John 4:19

Day 15

Pray that your husband will choose his friends wisely. Pray that God will bring him men who will encourage his accountability before God, and will not lead him into sin. [Prov. 13:20 Prov. 27:17]

Let me add this -Pray that first and foremost you and your husband would be BEST FRIENDS! Wow ya'll-when that happens -watch your relationship grow and go deeper than you imagined-it is an amazing place to be! You might wander what that looks like, it starts from a place of vulnerability and willingness to share with your husband about whatever is going on in your life FIRST before you call your mom, girlfriends or sisters. In Genesis 2:24 the Bible says that we leave our mother and father and CLEAVE unto our spouse. Make his friendship your number 1 friendship priority.

Also it truly is so important to surround yourself and your marriage with friends who encourage you in Christ and encourage you to be the man or woman God made you to be. I always feel SO refreshed after spending time fellowshipping with other like minded Christian women. Don't you want that type of fellowship for your man? Pray for your man's heart today that The Lord would bring him a true friend -a Friend that loves The Lord, that is relatable and real, not judgmental, but full of Grace and who won't sit by and just talk about the weather or work but someone who is interested in him as a person and interested in a real friendship as God designed for men to be for men! It's so awesome to DO LIFE with other believers especially when you are struggling through life or feel like you are just surviving! I am so thankful for my friends that build me up in love and encourage me but also when they do it in a REAL way-I want my husband to have that too!

I love how Paul writes to His brothers in Christ in a brotherly love -our men need that kind of brotherly love! Read all of this if you can Philemon 1:4-7 but here is the end of it "your love has given me great joy and encouragement, because you, brother, have refreshed the hearts of the saints"

Last thought! Whatever you want for your husband, whatever you want him to change or start or be different in or better at-instead of complaining-GO to the Father and intercede on your husband's behalf in prayer-the BEST thing you can ever do for your man!

James 5:13—Is -Is anyone among you suffering? Let him pray. Is anyone cheerful? Let him sing praise. Is anyone among you sick? Let him call for the elders of the church, and let them pray over him, anointing him with oil in the name of the Lord.

James 1:5—If any of you lacks wisdom let him ask God, who gives generously to all without reproach, and it will be given to him.

Day 16

Pray that your husband will choose healthy, God-honoring activities. Pray that he will not live in bondage to any questionable habits or hobbies, but that he will experience freedom in holiness as he yields to the Spirit's control. [1 Cor. 6:12-20,10:31

Yall let me encourage you to open up your Bible and read these passages and scriptures for yourselves! It is healing, encouraging, it is guidance, and teaching, rebuking, love, grace and God breathed words! 2 Timothy 3:16-17

YIKES on this area of prayer, this can range from all over the spectrum honestly and can also speak to our hearts, as well!

At first glance this prayer plea seems one that would be for maybe his eating or drinking but I'm pretty sure anything that is unhealthy to your body can be any sin! My brain is telling me dare I list them...my spirit says someone might need help identifying.... addiction of any kind-food, working out [yep good things can become addictions/idols too], sexual addictions, sports, hobbies, gambling, stress, alcohol, TV, politics, knowledge, money, education, job, business, friends, cigarettes, dip, partying, drugs] ok deep breath here I'm not in any way placing any judgment here it's when any of these things become our God, some are not bad things but can become bad when they are put before The Lord our God! Some of these ARE bad things, the Word clearly instructs those which are sin but the prayer here is for our husbands. We need to go before Father God with a pure heart, a heart that truly longs for freedom for our husbands-not because we want him to fit a certain mold or look better in the worlds eyes or in a nagging spirit but in a brokenness that truly desires healing and wholeness for our man.

"Father God, I lift up to you my "put your husband's name here", your precious son. Lord I know you love him more than I ever could and I know you have plans to use him and his story that brings you glory! I pray in the name of Jesus that you would free him from the bondage that holds him down in these areas (elaborate, list or however you feel you need) I pray that you would help him to come to you and lay them down at the foot of the cross and that he would desire to be pure and that he would Desire to bring you glory in every activity he does. In his eating, in his working out, in his job, in his education, in his sin, Father God I pray that he would put no other gods before you and that YOU would show him what a life like that looks like, that you would grant him peace and teach him balance and that you Father God would fill the void in his heart that he is trying to fill with all of these other things! I pray that you would return to him the joy of his salvation and that he would turn from his sin and that you would replace that with a longing to do your will and bring you glory! Thank you Father for the gift you have given me in my precious husband! He is yours! In JESUS NAME AMEN!

Day 17

Pray that your husband will enjoy his manliness as he patterns his life after Christ and strong men in the faith. Pray for his physical, emotional, mental, social and spiritual strength. [Eph. 3:16 Song of Solomon 5:10-16, Joshua 1:1-9]

Ok y'all -our man was made to be manly and brave and warrior like! I LOVE this passage in Song of Solomon where it describes her lover. How do we look at our man? Do we nag at him or tell him he needs to eat less or work out or maybe we don't say it but we definitely don't encourage him in his manliness either. Like I said before, it took me years to tell my husband how I really felt about him [out of fear]. Our man was made to be all of these things but they NEED to be affirmed by their bride, their beloved. They need to know that they satisfy us, that they are a good lover, that they are HOTT [yeah I just said that and spelled it that way], that they are strong, that we admire them for the things they are good at. They need to be thanked for the way they provide for us. If you don't feel any of those things about your husband, I urge you to go before the Father first with your heart 💔 father knows your heart, he knows why you don't see these things in your husband. We like to focus on what our husbands aren't for us and what they need to be. I did that for a LONG time when The Lord got a hold of My heart and said -how about you look in the mirror [in his sweet loving fatherly way 😑] ultimately I didn't like who I was and so I brought him down with me, I wounded him with my words or lack of words. I wounded him with my anger, bitterness and I wounded him out of my own wounds. God desires to restore our marriages y'all! I have watched him do a miracle in our lives. It wasn't easy or fast by any means, it took years out of my life and I hate that part [but it took so long because of me], but apparently I had a lot of impurities and he had to leave me on the fire for a long time. Yall he wants us to love our husbands and speak life and love into them. Maybe, honestly, your man isn't providing for you right now, maybe you are the bread winner or maybe it's always been a team thing financially or maybe you want to say it's just not his gift or his thing or maybe it's not yall's thing to say ooh baby you look HOTT! 😉 But no matter who he is, God has given him a gift or gifts, traits, characteristics, good, ect. And he desires to hear affirmation spoken to him and over him from his bride - find the GOOD that your man does have -FOCUS ON THE GOOD! Walk out in faith without fear of rejection or anything else and unconditionally and sacrificially show your man how amazing he is just because he is manly and brave and because you desire for him to be strengthened physically, emotionally mentally and spiritually because you want him to be what God created him to be!

To God be the Glory great things he has done!

Day 18

Pray that your husband will have an eternal perspective—living in light of eternity. Pray that he will reject materialism and temporal values and put God first in his life. [Matt. 6:33 Deut. 6:5 Eph. 5:15-16 Ps. 90:12]

This is an area you may need to sit on for a couple days. There is a real battle going on in our souls-a battle between the flesh and the spirit and the Eternal things and worldly/material things! The battle is hard, daunting and real. This specific prayer convicts my heart, as I have struggled with the materialistic battle for so long. Here is what most of us have found -the world leaves us empty, always wanting more, never satisfied, comparing ourselves and our things to others, stealing our joy and feeling like a failure. That isn't how God intended us to live our life. God wants you, me and each of our husbands to walk in his will and live in light of eternity. There we find acceptance, we find the validation we desire, the peace that surpasses worldly understanding, and the love that covers a multitude of sins. The Lord is just leading me to pray today!

She Does Him Good   By: Haley Bates

Father God-I come humbly before your throne, I am interceding for my husband and myself Father that you would help us throw off all that hinders us and entangles me and him into sin. I ask that you would remove from me and my husband the desires of this world and the desire to have and want and think about materialistic things. Father God I ask that you would fill us up to the brim with your unfailing love and that we would abound in Love as Christ loves and that we would desire to do things that are eternal. Show us Lord what that looks like, walked out in this world. Father, help us to find our identity in you and to sit humbly at your feet as you guide us on how to live in your will. I especially lift up my husband to you right now, today at this very moment that you would wrap your arms around him and that today he would feel your presence and that he would begin to seek you and that he would hear your voice leading him into you and away from the materialistic and the temporary things of this world. I pray that his affection would first be for you and that you would show him how to live eternally one step, one day at a Time. You love him so much and you created him for your glory and you know my man's heart. Help me to not hinder the work that you may be doing in his heart or what you may be stirring up in his spirit. Help me to live out your love for him and to show grace for him and to love him like Jesus loves me. Help me to get out of the way so that he can see you. Father God thank you for my precious gift in my husband. Guide him to your heart today! In JESUS NAME AMEN!

Day 19

Pray that your husband will yield his mind and thoughts to the Lord. Pray that he will not entertain immoral or impure thoughts, and that he will resist the temptation to indulge in pornography. Pray also that God would help you fulfill your husband's sexual desires [as we discussed previously] and pray that you would be readily available to fulfill his desires and needs.
[Matthew 5:28, 1 Corinthians 6:18-20, psalms 119:37]

the prudent see danger and take refuge, but the simple keep going and suffer for it. Proverbs 27:12

Deep breaths here-are you still with me? This is such a HARD issue for me. Maybe you have experienced pain from pornography or just your man maybe having impure thoughts about someone else or maybe you haven't. I hope you haven't but this is a very REAL issue for men. Pornography and the adulterous women are all readily available. Pornography is a lot of times free and easy to hide! Even wonderful Christian men have struggled with these issues. It's still a hard subject to talk about for me, God is asking me to go there and to be available to you if you need to talk about it or if you need prayer. It's a delicate issue but it needs to be openly and honestly discussed and women need to be on guard and aware, but not live in fear. The light needs to be brought to the darkness of the world of pornography.

The light shines in the darkness and the darkness doesn't understand it (John 1:5)

I have witnessed the destruction of men and marriages from pornography. If you think this doesn't apply to you, I urge you to at least pray that if it isn't a temptation now for your husband, Pray that it never will be. Pornography can be an addiction just like drugs or alcohol and it seems harmless, but I assure you it is not harmless. I still don't understand all of the whys behind pornography, even though I've heard or read most all of them, but What I do know is that our Father God is faithful to restore that which has been broken and that he is near to the brokenhearted and he binds up our wounds -AMEN! [Psalm 34:18] He is also faithful to rid a man of this powerful stronghold that the deceiver has on him and make him clean and free from the bondage of this sin and the bondage it may have on his life.

If you have struggled in this area or have battled or are going through this battle and you need someone to talk to or to pray for you. Please let me know. Let God in the hidden places of your heart today-let his healing touch cover those caves and tear down those walls. He wants you and/or your husband freed from the bondage that entangles us, suffocates us and traps us.

Day 20

Pray that your husband will be patient and a man of peace. . [Rom. 14:19 Ps. 34:14, Philippians 4:6-7, 1 Corinthians 14:33, Isaiah 48:18, Psalm 119:165]

Ahh.... After yesterday's challenge this One is so lovely!!! Praying for peace ☺ However, You may still be dealing with yesterday's issue or you may be done with it, but a sweet sister of mine brought up a really great Point that I just want to touch on-amidst the pornography thing from yesterday. Pornography really does attack women too ya'll but it's disguised so well. Just Because it isn't blatant pictures or videos of men - the things we allow in our minds, as well, must be filtered and Philippians 4:8 must be applied to all things-there is a very popular book turned movie which I haven't read but have heard a lot about and it is from what I understand pornography for the woman's imagination. We must be on Guard friends and we can't think for one minute that we are not vulnerable to attack in this area as well. Our men need our fully committed hearts and imaginations too. They want our fantasies, they want to Know how to romance us, but if we fill our minds up with pornography, we can't ever get to the intimacy level that we truly desire with our man! If you feel like you are distant from The Lord or no matter how much you are praying these prayers, you still feel distance- psalms 139:23-24 says search me oh God and Know my heart -see if there is any offensive way in me -that's a Hard verse to say when you Know there are things In your heart you don't want to talk about. I remember being in a place where I had some serious junk in my heart and I didn't really want The Lord To search my heart because I knew it wasn't pretty in there but guess what -then we don't move Forward, we Don't move in the direction that God has for us, for his greater Purpose And really the desires of our heart can't be fulfilled until we can intimately walk with our Savior and know that we have left no "known" stone unturned in our heart and that we can repent and turn from our wicked ways and declare our need for a savior and then y'all BEST PART stay with me-coming back around to today's prayer subject THEN y'all can we TRULY experience the peace that we long for that only he can provide in us and in our husbands lives.

One of my husband's favorite verses

Create in me a pure heart, O God, and renew a steadfast spirit within me. Psalm 51:10

Father God hear our hearts, you know our hearts you know if We are Ready for our own heart to be searched and if We are ready Lord we ask that you would go to work in our hearts and in our husbands heart and clean out The junk. Help us to get on our knees before the throne of you our GRACIOUS GOD for there is where we receive your mercy and you will cleanse us and give Us strength to repent from our sins and you will fill us up with your peace - a peace that onely comes From A Pure heart, for your word says blessed are the pure in heart for they will SEE you! Lord we want to see you! We lift up our husbands and our own hearts to you and we ask that you would Rid of us of our junk, our sin, our shame, our anger, our bitterness and envy and Father God we ask that you would forgive Us for each of these places where we have failed you and we humbley ask you in your mercy, to Replace Those parts of our hearts and our husbands hearts with your peace and your abounding love and light! In JESUS NAME AMEN!

Day 21

Pray that your husband will not give in to anger, but will allow the Holy Spirit to control his responses. [Rom. 14:19 Ps. 34:14]

There are 3 revelations I have had in the last few years about anger, First is that you cannot react to anger-although this is the HARDEST thing for me and most everyone. When you read through the next part, you might find it easier to not react so- **Second** when someone reacts in anger my initial thought has changed from just wanting to defend myself or react back or lose it myself **TO instead**- having compassion for them because I realize that they are most likely speaking out of a Wounded area or out of a guilty spirit and I begin to wonder what is going on in their heart? I think that is how our Father sees us and when we can begin to see people [especially our husbands] in this way, it will allow us to respond instead of react. Another thing about the reacting issue that I found, for years in our relationship it seemed like we would go round and round and never deal with the root issue. Does anyone else experience this? you know the cycle- It goes something like this- first person is hurting and says something in anger, The other person only hears the part they said in anger and reacts and starts defending and throwing daggers and then first person reacts to those daggers and you end up escalating so far you don't even remember what started the whole dang thing and it's so frustrating because ultimately first person was just hurting, wounded or already feeling guilty about something and if second person would just respond with listening and really trying to figure out or even notice that there was a deeper issue - a heart issue, I think it would help us all respond more like Jesus! WHEW! That wore me out! It may take some re-reading or we could go straight to the Word of God-

TRUTH: A gentle answer truly does turn away wrath and a harsh one stirs up anger! Proverbs 15:1

Again SPEAK LIFE !! If it is you that struggles with anger, look deeper into your wounds and hurts and if you need help figuring that out or talking them out in a non reactive atmosphere, I or many other Christian friends would be happy to listen. If it's your husband that struggles with anger, first and foremost y'all PRAY for him daily in this issue that he would be filled up with the Holy Spirit and also that you would seek out his heart and the real issues would be exposed and in a compassionate way you would begin to help him work through them all the while, Covering him in prayer!

I love this verse-

a gift given in secret soothes anger!

Proverbs 21:14

The gift done in secret for your man, whether it be prayer or anything that may build him Up WILL pacify anger!!

Can I get an AMEN?? To God be the Glory!

Day 22

Pray that your husband in his greatest times of stress, will find joy and peace in his relationship with God. [Neh. 8:10 Prov. 17:22 Ps. 16:11, Isaiah 40:29-31]

Remember when you pray to be SPECIFIC for your man! Consider what he may have going on today in his schedule, in his work, a new client, a new project, a jerk boss, cows getting out ☺ [just a guess on what might be a problem for ranchers] maybe it's an overwhelming amount of orders to finish, looking for a job and not being able to find one, whatever he may be facing today -Consider the weight that he is carrying, consider his burden! In the midst of your prayer for him today, be specific for his needs, for his heart, for his stress, his physical reactions to stress, bind Satan from attacking your marriage today and adding to his stress. Do something sweet for him today, do or say something that speaks to where he is at, that lets him know you are interested in him, concerned for him or just want to be there for him. I hesitate to use the Golden Rule because it comes back around to self and in this we should try to be selfless but if it helps with perspective- truly can you imagine if your husband did all of the above for YOU- how much more would you want to shower him with your love, with kisses, with who knows what else we are all hungry for someone [especially and should be our mat☺ see our needs, to lift us up the Father, to truly care about what we have going on specifically that day. We all [including your man] we want to be KNOWN! If you don't know what is going on in his life-get to know your man today! Desire to know him; from his heart, to his stressful tasks at work. Let him know you are in his corner rooting for HIM! I pray that the Father would reveal something to you today-something that would change your marriage forever in the way of The Lord and that you would consider your man as a gift from God today. I know how hard this is to hear when you are going through a really hard time or you just aren't feeling super close or you are angry or hurt, but I promise just teeny steps toward him will begin to break down walls and break bondage. Start chipping away at the hardened hearts in you or your spouse and ask The Lord for his help in wanting and desiring to be these things to and for your husband! He will begin to soften hearts and HE IS STILL MOVING!

Ezekiel 36:26 ESV

And I will give you a new heart, and a new spirit I will put within you. And I will remove the heart of stone from your flesh and give you a heart of flesh

John 14:27 Peace I leave with you my peace I give you. I do not give to you as the world gives. Do not let your hearts be troubled and do not be afraid.

Day 23

Pray that your husband will be encouraged today or be an encouragement to other men in the name of Jesus! [Phil. 2:14-16, 1 Thessalonians 5:11, Col. 3:13, Galatians 6:2, Eph. 4:29]

The Lord pressed on my heart to change the direction which I had planned on for this day and go in this direction. As a friend and I were talking, I was feeling burdened with the lack of Godly encouragement and fellowship men have with other men. We women know how much we need and long for fellowship with "our girls" our men need it too! Unfortunately it gets confused with a longing for worldly things but I truly believe deep in their hearts they long for a brotherhood of believers-that they can be real with, do life with, encourage each other in and speak truth and pray for one another-I'm not talking about a bunch of overly religious men in suits or monk like outfits hanging out praying all day long-but y'all- just guys getting together and being REAL and encouraging each other just like we need. This does go back to day 15 When we prayed for Godly friends and influences. Instead of complaining about their friends, lets pray for their friends and whoever they are around daily that they would be used to encourage or be encouraged in The Lord by other men [specifically I say men-it's not healthy for them to be encouraged by other women] pray that you would also encourage his heart and that if he doesn't have time or options for friends that The Lord would reveal how YOU can be his best friend! Send him a text or call right now and encourage him and tell him something that speaks life to his heart, bones and soul!

And let us consider how to stir up one

another to love and good works and let us not give up meeting together as some are in the habit of doing! Hebrews 10:24-25

Don't you think this picture [of my precious boys] says a lot about our men's hearts they just want another superhero buddy friend to walk through life with [Matthew 18:3-4]

Day 24

Pray that your husband will recognize the lies of the Enemy in his life. Pray that his attitudes and actions will be guided by the truth as he brings his thoughts into captivity to the Word of God. [John 8:42-47, 2 Cor. 10:3-5,]

I've always been a pursuer of truth! It's just always been important to me. I even told Josh very early in our relationship that I hated liars- Wow -my perspective was so skewed because Hl we are all liars at some Point or another. We can be so dang judgmental you know? And so wrapped up in "hating" things, people, ect because of their choices or sin. JOHN 8:7 -when we truly learn to put on the "glasses of compassion" for the sinner [which we ALL are] we begin to hurt for them or what they may be going through or how they may be being deceived by the Father of Lies- that was truly my burden when I started this little "challenge/project" to help us change our stinking glasses or put some on for the first time. The beginning healing in our marriage came when we actually separated and It was a sad, dark time and God got a hold of my heart and he began to show me my husband through his eyes of GRACE, MERCY & COMPASSION- and our healing process began. I screwed it up I'm sure MANY more times but slowly I began to get in the habit of seeing him through the lens of grace and I hurt for his battles and his struggles and the deception and yall hear me on this because this is huge -**I began to**

hate the deceiver instead of the deceived. [sit on that one for a while if you need to]

Also, sometimes being a pursuer of truth can be painful because you think you are ready for truth but sometimes you have no idea what God has in store for you. Some of these subjects are tough y'all and I don't want to apologize for them but they may hit nerves and the Holy Spirit is moving in marriages-there is a war being waged for your marriage daily! I urge you to put on the armor of God [Eph. 6:14] first thing in the armor of God y'all-the **BELT OF TRUTH** around your waist! Ask The Lord to reveal truth to your husband and to you -and ask The Lord to guide you both in speaking truth and walking in truth today and everyday!

TO GOD BE THE GLORY! ❤

Day 25

Pray that your husband will practice forgiveness in your relationship and with others. Pray that he will recognize any roots of bitterness, and yield any resentment and unforgiving attitudes to the Lord. [Eph. 4:32 Heb. 12:15]

I feel like this is something few of us have probably prayed for -for our husbands. So much of ALL of mankind's anger, issues, addictions, wounds to others and bad choices stem from a root issue, usually a wounded place in our heart. One that we haven't dealt with and some of us may not even know we have it and sometimes we just really have to pray that God would reveal what the root of the issue stems from. Your precious husband, looking at him from the Lords eyes and having compassion on his heart; What did he go through, what hurt him badly, where did the world wound him, maybe it was in school, maybe a bully, maybe his parents or another family member, maybe it was you who hurt him or cheated on him, maybe he's a child of divorce or lost someone close to him, maybe it was being deployed and seeing awful things that no one should have to see, maybe it was an accident or a tragedy, maybe he never felt good enough, maybe his parents didn't express their love, affection, affirmation of him or recognize his worth. What has your husband walked through that he keeps hidden deep down in his heart? Yall he may not even want to remember or want to go there so tread gently in this area, but we all carry around baggage and we [men especially] cover it up with all kinds of things like all the aholics ,work-Aholic, alcoholic, drugs, being an upstanding businessman, looking for success in the worlds eyes, adultery, pornography, video games, money, power, accolades, monetary possessions, Ect. See a lot of the things we have prayed for him not to be or the struggle he has comes from a deeper rooted issue. He needs his bride to walk beside him and look at him with the "glasses of compassion." Look at him as The Lord sees him-While, yes, he was made to be this brave, strong, fearless leader for us as our family, we can't have double standards for him and expect that he doesn't have inward struggles like we do. We live in a fallen world, a world where we have all been beaten down and wounded at sometime in our life. How would we want to be treated? What if your husband responded lovingly to one of your emotional outbursts with compassion and spoke tenderly to us and held us while the onion peeled back one layer at a time? Wow! I think most all of us would love that. Sometimes your man just needs to put his sword down and deal with his wounds. Be ready to listen and love and hurt with him-and if he isn't ready to talk about it or deal with it -that's ok too, but be sensitive and PRAY that he would share in his time but most Importantly that The Lord would begin to work in the hard, Covered and wounded places of your man's heart and that your husband would begin to forgive whoever hurt him and he would be freed of the burden he is carrying around.

Finally, all of you, be like-minded, be sympathetic, love one another, be compassionate and humble! Do not repay evil with evil or insult with insult! On the contrary, repay evil with blessing! 1 Peter 3:8-9

Day 26

Pray that your husband will know for certain who he is and that he will find his identity in Christ. [Colossians 3:9-10, Gal. 3:26, 2 Corinthians 3:1&1 Peter 2:9]

I was blessed to grow up in a home where my mom made sure we talked about and knew WHO we were as individuals and my parents allowed us to be the individual that God made us to be. My mom's famous quote, some of you may know is

"REMEMBER WHO YOU ARE AND WHOSE YOU ARE!"

One of the best non-scripture quotes that I have clung to many times in my life. When the world tried to tell me I was something else or I began to sway this way or that-I had to ask myself and remind myself -who are you ? And whose are you? The answer for me Is this: Who I am is completely because of WHOSE I AM. I feel very blessed to have learned that at such a young age, but there are SO so many, especially men [because this isn't something a lot of people sit around and talk about with boys or men] that don't know WHO they are. They've never dove in and searched that out or they merely answer to the names that the world calls them. Some of you may know my story about the name The Lord gave me. Josh and I went to an amazing retreat several years ago, we were asked to ask The Lord to reveal what name He calls you, Not the names that the world calls you [ie fat, skinny, smart, average, dumb, athletic, ugly, stubborn, wild, crazy, pretty, rich, successful, stupid Ect]. I prayed and cried out to The Lord in my little hotel room and journaled and almost audibly I heard The Lord call me Beloved! One of the most beautiful and defining moments in my walk with The Lord. The name he calls me is what defines me now. I tell you this story to say 2 Things, 1-I hope that you will take some time to ask The Lord to reveal to you the name he calls you and them claim it and walk in it and let go of the names the world calls you and 2-y'all pray this for your husband and build him up [as I've said a few times]

Be ready to help him discover his true identity in Christ-help him throw off the names and the "identity" the world has called him and definitely don't add to that false identity by labeling him or defining him or his worth by something that is of this world. Pray that he would hear The Lord speak to him and call Him by name and that the Lord would remind him who he is!

For we are his workmanship, created in Christ Jesus for good works, which God prepared beforehand, that we should walk in them. Ephesians 2:10If you get a chance, check out this awesome video of the song "remind me who I am" https://m.youtube.com/watch?vQSIVjjY80u8

Day 27

Pray for your husband's discouragement, depression, anxiety or stress. Pray that he would be able to lay these things at the Fathers feet and that his burden would be light and be free to serve The Lord, his family and his job with joy and peace.

[2 Corinth. 4:8-9, 2 Cor.. 12:9-10, Phil. 4:6-7, 19, John 10:1, Ok I'm going to stop because I could keep going -so many verses on these issues.]

Ladies-we are not the only ones that struggle with discouraged hearts, stressed out, overworked, being underappreciated, depression, anxiety and self image issues. We focus so much sometimes on our own Issues and our needs that our man is walking alone through his issues or masking them, denying them, hiding them or anesthetizing them. We get mad at him because he's distant or not there for us but when was the last time we dug into him and asked him about how he is feeling, truly interested in his day and not just so we can tell him about our day? Obviously praying for him daily is amazing and helpful but being interested in him and **living out** the love, concern and compassion we are praying about is what will speak volumes to him. Giving him a scripture or texting him your prayer may be just what his heart needs today. Ask him how you can help him or what you can do to lighten his load-he might laugh lol or he might be shocked but I promise it will mean a lot to him.

I waited patiently for The Lord; he turned to me and heard my cry. He lifted me out of the miry pit, out of the mud and the mire; he set my feet upon the rock and gave me a firm place to stand!

Psalm 40:1-2

The Lord God said "it is not good for man to be alone. I will make a HELPER suitable for him."

Genesis 2:18

Day 28

Pray for your husband's protection, physical, mental, emotional and spiritual. [Psalm 23:4, psalm 5:11, Ezra 9:9, 1 Cor. 10:13, Col. 2:6-7]

This is probably a more common prayer that we say for our husbands and while I have tried to touch on some prayers that we aren't used to saying-this one is still very important to pray over and over for our husbands! Pray that The Lord will protect him from harm's way and accidents and protect his life. Learn to look at certain closed doors as Gods protection over your marriage and maybe even his life. When Josh tried out for the fire department for 8 years and never got in - we were discouraged, but The Lord began to show me to be thankful for each closed door and that I had no idea what Father was protecting us or him from. He could have been protecting his life or he could have been protecting our marriage. Pray that The Lord will also protect him spiritually against the spiritual battles of this world that we have discussed [eph. 6:12] pray that he would prepare for battle and that he would daily put on the armor of God. Ask The Lord to protect him from temptation-instead of living in fear, ask The Lord to take him out of situations which may tempt him to be unfaithful or to not have integrity or cheat. Pray that The Lord would protect him from people that drag him down or attack him verbally or physically in his job or his ministry or his calling in life. Ask The Lord to put a -not a hedge, let's go with a stinking concrete wall with barbed wire fence of protection around his car, around his body, around his heart and his mind. Lift your man up to The Lord. Release the worry or fear you may have about your husband-lay it at the foot of the cross and give your husband to The Lord. Exchange your fears for his peace and never stop lifting up your man to the

Father. He is so special to you and this is the BEST gift you can give him. Let him know today how special he is to you and how thankful you are to walk through this life with him by your side! Don't waste today, you never know if you or your loved one has tomorrow but you can make everyday beautiful when you have a thankful heart! Let us live like Christ everyday while we have the chance in this FREE country! May we extend love in every word we say and every action we take so that others will come to know our savior and so that we will have no regrets. May we cherish each day as a blessing and be thankful for this beautiful life that we have. I don't watch news, we don't have cable or even regular channels so I'm in the dark a lot but I've recently been informed and heartbroken over what I'm hearing is going on in the world, y'all we have it SO good and SO easy compared to the rest of the world and we complain and grumble take it for granted-I was at a newsboys concert recently and -one of the coolest things I've heard was -"there are people over there dying for Christ -in AMERICA we are barely LIVING for Christ!"

FATHER -help us to LIVE for you in ALL we do.

Yes we are busy, crazy, exhausted, stressed but we have brought most of that on ourselves. I constantly over plan my week and my budget and I wake up feeling stressed like crazy. Come to me sweet girl-he's calling out -oh and sweet girl-those were your plans -not mine. I have to stop ask The Lord to forgive me and to help me know what to let Go of today and be reminded that unless my to do list lines up with his, it is not eternal and it should not be my focus! Humbled at his feet!

"Give thanks in all circumstances for this is Gods will for you in Christ Jesus."

1 Thessalonians 5:18

Day 29

Pray for your husband's walk with The Lord. Pray that he would be on fire for Christ and that he would be a man of prayer and that he would seek Gods word daily. Pray that he will be courageous to be bold for Christ, throwing off what others may think of him in the process.
[Romans 1:16, 2 Tim. 1:8-9, Hosea 6:1-3]

I pray that you are seeing a difference in your marriage and that God is working in you and your husband's heart. Some of you and your husbands have been Christians a long time and have heard these things many times -some of you are new believers and some may be somewhere in the middle but I believe The Lord is calling all of us and our husbands by name -he wants us To break free from being luke-warm Christians and instead to be on fire for Christ.

I encourage you to stay in the word daily, not out of duty but out of desire to know The Lord deeper, stay near to The Lord in your prayer life because we are all susceptible to being in the habit of being too busy and all of these wonderful things that we have talked about will fall away and we will forget what The Lord wants to do in our marriage-just like the Israelites who wandered the desert for 40 years - 40 years y'all because they so quickly forgot all the miracles The Lord had brought them through, they took for granted what The Lord had done for them and how he provided and restored them. We see this time and time again in the Bible and we shake our heads and think "how can they not see what he did for them?" It's so easy to see that from outside the situation looking in, yet we are guilty of it too. We so quickly forget all that The Lord has done for us and we get so wrapped up in minor details that didn't go right for us or that we can't get something we want, feeling like we are being wronged, being a generation of entitlement or comparing ourselves, the list goes on and on.

Father help us not to forget what you have done for us, help us to remember the miracles,
The provisions and restorations you have done in our lives and in our marriages.

Ultimately he wants us to repent and turn from our wicked ways so that we can walk with him and he can restore our hearts and our marriages, he has so much patience with us and is willing to go through this refining process with us over and over again! Continue to Pray for your husband to desire to walk with The Lord and to be courageous, to declare the truths of the word with other men and to be clothed in the fruits of the spirits that they would shine off of his face.

"But in your hearts revere Christ as Lord. Always be prepared to give an answer to everyone who asks you to give the reason for the hope that you have. But do this with gentleness and respect." 1 Peter 3:15

"Be strong and courageous. Do not fear or be in dread of them, for it is the Lord your God who goes with you. He will not leave you or forsake you." Deuteronomy 31:6

"But now thus says the Lord, he who created you, O Jacob, he who formed you, O Israel: "Fear not, for I have redeemed you I have called you by name, you are mine."
Isaiah 43:1

Day 30

Pray for your husband to be your FEARLESS, STRONG, BRAVE, COURAGEOUS & LOVING LEADER and that you would ALLOW him to be that for you and your family! [Col. 3:18, 1 Peter 3:7, 1 Cor. 11:3, Gen. 2:23, eph. 4:32, 1 Cor. 16:3, Psalm 27:3]

Whoa sorry for all the verses, last day -trying to squeeze in as many as possible ☺

Now that we have prayed for our husbands in so many ways, today lets lift him up to the Father to be the man, the fearless leader, that God made him to be. Let's get out of the way of what God wants to do in our men. If we let go of control, which face it, we have issues with control, I believe we will see our men be the bold, Courageous men of God that we so desire. Eve took over control in the Garden, took things into her own hands, literally-haha! But the devil deceived her by telling her if she ate the fruit from the forbidden tree, then she would be like God. Don't you know he speaks the same kind of lies to us- -he says- hey you need to take care of this yourself, you need to take things into your own hands, don't count on a man, you don't need anyone's help, you don't need to submit to a man, stand up for your rights, you deserve to buy that, your husband won't know or your husband won't ever do it so you might as well, He's lazy and not a leader, ect, ect. Guess what? When we listen to the "father of Lies" we, not only are being deceived just like Eve was, but we are suffocating our husbands in the process from being the fearless leader that God created them to be. When Eve decided to "take things into her own hands" Adam was paralyzed! He didn't do squat about it or remind her that "hey God said not to do that." He just ATE the fruit and went along with it! HELLO!! I think we sometimes do crazy things and just hope our men will step up and call us out or stand up to us or speak truth into us. I know I do and when my man speaks truth into my life and calls out the lies I'm believing from the great Deceiver -it might sting a bit at first

but I it and I desire that from him. I believe our men are capable of so much more but we tend to suffocate them or we don't trust that they are capable. With our prayers for them and their encouraging and supportive bride at their sides-I believe they are capable of more than we could ever have imagined. I'm not talking about letting them do the "manly" things the world has labeled should be a man's job-like fixing our cars, changing our oil, managing the money, or bringing home the bacon. It's far deeper than these things and honestly there is no where written that these are a man's job anyway. Marriage is a team and woman was created to be a "suitable helper" [gen. 2:18] for men. Although the world has definitely skewed this idea [as it has with most things] We constantly complain about him not helping us out around the house, but WOW we were made to be HIS helper? God designed US to be HIS helper, not the other way around. [Sit on that one for a minute]. Let him walk into the dark first [of life], if you will, encouraging him and being his cheering section all along the way, asking him what do you need? How can I help you today? Let your man lead you into the great unknown, this great adventure of Life, Love and Marriage!

We have prayed for many issues for our husbands and hopefully our own lives during this journey. I pray that your journey has been eye opening and that The Lord has spoken tenderly to your heart. I pray that you have been able to see your husband with the "glasses of compassion" and that you will remember to put them on daily. Thank you for being a part of this challenge and being patient with me and having grace on me with typos and other mistakes-thank you for letting me Share my heart with you. It hasn't been easy for me to share some of these very deep places of my heart, but I know God called me to do this and I know that every word that was good came from the Holy Spirit. Rest in Jesus. Stay at the foot of the cross!! To God be the Glory FOREVER AMEN!

Humbled at his feet,

Haley

About the Author:

Haley is first and foremost a Christ follower, a sinner saved by God's Grace! She lives in Poteet, Texas with her husband, Josh. They have 3 children, Hallie Grace, Jacob & Caleb who are beautiful on the inside and out. Haley is a homeschooling momma and owns BELOdesigns Jewelry, where she makes hand stamped jewelry designed to honor God and remind us of God's love and what is truly important in life.

She is passionate about the restoration the Lord can do in the hearts of women and marriages.
Check out her website www.belodesignsjewelry.com and feel free to contact her at haleydbates@gmail.com.

Lightning Source UK Ltd.
Milton Keynes UK
UKHW020637280519
343376UK00011B/368/P

9 781320 661492